THE PROPHETIC WARRIORS

Other books by Raphael Grant:

Another Level of Prayer

Still Standing

Principles of Purpose and Adversity

Breaking Satanic Cycles

Strategic Prayer

Enemy at the Gate

THE PROPHETIC WARRIORS

Army of Fearless Warriors

RAPHAEL GRANT

Library of Congress Control Number: 2021910813
ISBN: Hardcover   978-1-6641-7706-2
                   Softcover   978-1-6641-7705-5
                   eBook   978-1-6641-7704-8

Print information available on the last page.

Rev. date: 05/27/2021

To order additional copies of this book, contact:
Xlibris
844-714-8691
www.Xlibris.com
Orders@Xlibris.com
830121

Contents

I am dedicating this book to my boys Zuriel and Zephan,

I love you guys so much,you are my inspiration,

and also to you my queen, my best friend Aretha,

forever in love with you.

Tested Generation

The undercover generation is the last generation before Christ returns. This is the chosen army that will herald the second coming of the Lord Jesus Christ; that is why they cannot fail or afford to make mistakes. As a result of that, this last generation, which is the end-time army of God has been tested, tried in every area of life to ascertain their fitness by God for the end-time commission.

Tests are recommended for elevation. And no teacher or masters give his students or servants tests without a purpose. This test is designed to redefine the army, to mold character, to uproot those that can be uprooted, and to clean and polish for the master's use. Tests are to prove someone's ability. God tests his children to prove them so that He can promote them.

A test is a set of questions, exercises, or practical activities to measure someone's skill, ability, or knowledge. A test is a difficult situation in which the qualities of someone or something are clearly shown. To stand the test of time is to be good enough, strong enough to last for a long time.

The glory of gold is revealed when it's tried with fire; it is the fire that brings out the glory of the gold. Otherwise the glory will be hidden in its rawness without the ability to glitter.

Trials refer to a process of testing to find out whether something works effectively and is safe. It is a short period during which you use something or employ someone to find whether they are satisfactory for a particular purpose or job.

God has tried this army to examine their faithfulness and ability. Afflictions can be trials. God can allow the devil to try his children, as in the case of Job, to prove the devil to try his children, as in the case of Job, to prove to the devil these are the untouchables.

Joseph was tried by word to perfect his character for the mission and assignment God has for him.

"Until the time came to fulfil his dreams, the Lord tested Joseph's character" (Ps. 105:19).

Joseph had a dream; it wasn't just a dream, it was his divine mandate, but it wasn't just going to come to pass without trials. He had to lose his coat of many colors through trials to be qualified for the royal regalia. There are so many holding on to their coats of many colors because they think this is all there is but not this army, not this generation. They let go what must be let go in order to have and to receive what God has for them. There is higher, bigger, and better than what they let go!

Joseph needed to be in the pit to learn that his deliverance and salvation is none other than God, learning to trust him even when you're at the bottom. He needed to go through the trial of servanthood in Potiphar's house to teach how to serve and to earn humanity.

Joseph went to prison to learn administration and also how to manage people, not in a pleasant place, but that is where he got his master's in MBA.

To former saints or should I say, the saints of old have trials of mocking and scourging, yes and of chains and imprisonment (Heb. 11:35–38). Jesus Christ was baptized with the baptism of suffering and shame. Each of us has his own cross (or price as some call it to bear or pay).

You cannot be a part of this army without the required sacrifice God expects from you.

Obedience is better and sacrifice is a fact. The right sacrifice is what God wants from you and because of your love for God.

Your faith will be tried to prove the genuineness of it. When you overcome, you will receive praise, honor, and glory at the revelation of Jesus Christ (1 Pet. 1:7).

> Beloved, think it not strange concerning the fiery trial
> which is to try you, as though some strange thing happen

unto you; but rejoice in as much as yet partakers of Christ's suffering, that, when his glory shall be revealed, ye may be good also with exceeding joy.

If ye be reproached for the name of Christ happy are ye, for the spirit of Glory and of God resteth upon you, on their part he is evil spoken of, but on your part, he is glorified.

But, let none of your suffer as a murder or as their, or as evildoer, or as busy body in other men's matter.

Yet if any man suffer as a Christian let him not be ashamed; but let him glorify God on this behalf. (1 Pet. 4:12–15)

If you are reproached for the name of Christ, blessed are you for the spirit of glory and of God rests upon you. Count it all joy when you fall into various trials, knowing that the testing of your faith produces patience.

"But let patience have its perfect work, that you may be perfect and complete lacking nothing" (James 1:2–4).

But let none of you suffer as an evildoer or as busy body in other people's matters.

Temptation is an attempt by the devil to persuade someone to do something by making it seem attractive, but God will not allow temptation that is greater than you to come your way.

"No temptation has overtaken you except such as is common to man, but God is Faithful; who will not allow you to be tempted beyond what you are able.

"If you encounter temptation, God will also make the way of escape, that you may be able to bear it." (1 Cor. 10:13)

Any temptation that comes your way is common to man; others have experienced it.

It is in the affliction and in the furnace of affliction that faith brightens; gold is not gold until it has gone through fire. What makes gold valuable and appealing is the glistening but is the fire that refines it.

"All the days of my appointed time, will I wait, till my change come" (Job 14:4).

"But he knoweth the way I take, when he hath tried me, I shall come forth as gold" (Job 23:10).

"Though he slay me, yet will trust him, but I will maintain mine ways before him" (Job 13:15).

This is an army the devil cannot touch this army is resolute in their faith and walk with God. They love God.

The Power of Humility

We are living in the day when men and women of God are fishing for money, fame, and stardom, instead of fishing for men. Today is all about titles—big titles—wanting to have a big name and they want to be addressed with big titles. Some call themselves *super apostle, apostle general.* Some create their own titles as to how people should address them. All of this is a result of pride, ego, and self-esteem, and the bottom line is pride, self-exaltation. We are living in a day, where people have to be addressed by their titles, and if they are not, they get offended and furious. I remember how countless people have asked me when am I going to be consecrated as a bishop because they feel everybody is a bishop, and they don't understand why I am not because that is their lifestyle now.

It is not about who we are, it is about who he is; having that in mind keeps us humble. Sometimes it is astonishing when you hear or listen to men of God, so-called preaching or teaching, is all about them and ask you to listen to them. You ask yourself, where is Christ in all of this? To listen as a child of God, we are what we are, and we are who we are because of Jesus. This is why the undercover generation must know that the honor, the glory, and sometimes the accolades are because of the reflection of Christ on us, not ourselves.

One of the things I do constantly whenever the Lord sends me to is to always talk about where he picked me from. I wasn't the best. I wasn't the most educated. I wasn't the most articulate, and certainly not the most handsome, but he decided to use me for His divine agenda and purpose. If that is not humbling enough, then what else.

"Ye have not chosen me, but I have chosen you, and ordained you, that ye should go and bring forth fruit, and that your fruit should remain; that whatsoever ye shall ask of the Father in my name, He may give it to you" (John 15:16).

According as he has chosen us in with everything within us, we must cultivate and pursue the brand of humility that matters most, the kind that defines a lifetime of walking with God.

True greatness is not in our accomplishments and is also not in our achievements and is certainly not in our conquest, but is in the fact that without him, we can do nothing. That is where true greatness lives.

When we take our minds from the human audience, we are so often preoccupied with and remind us of the one observer, our only sovereign and Savior, whose attention can be captured by a heart and life that display genuine humility. Our desire for true greatness is in God's eye. It will increase and overflow in a life of true humility.

Let me just say something here and now I am not writing on this chapter of humility because I have attained it. I am not writing on humility because I am an authority. I am a proud man pursuing humility by the grace of God because is a necessary ingredient for the end-time army.

I am just a fellow pilgrim walking with you on the path set for us by our humble and Savior Jesus Christ. I am only addressing you with confidence in the great and gracious God who has promised to give grace to the humble (see James 4:6; 1 Pet. 5:5); that promise forms the heart of this chapter.

It doesn't matter who you are your status, your age, and your vocation. One most thing you must know humility is our greatest friend, and pride is our greatest foe.

Genuine humility requires a radical transformation of the heart and mind. True power is attainable only through humility in Christ Jesus. Where there is pride, power is lost, but where there is humility, power is attained. To weaken pride, we must pursue humility aggressively.

We live in a culture that applauds and so often rewards the proud, a world quick to admire and clap for the prideful, a world anxious to bestow the label *powerful* on these small individuals.

I read a book entitled *Good to Great* by Jim Collins, an amazing book for every leader. There was a couple I learned from the book which typifies humility. The book is driven by a question. Can a good company become a great company, and if so, how? To find the answer, Collins and a team of researchers spent five years studying eleven corporations that had made the leap from being merely good companies to being great ones.

Collins identified two specific character qualities shared by the CEO of these good to great companies.

The first was no surprise. These men possessed incredible professional will; they were driven, willing to endure anything to make their companies successful. The second trait these leaders had in common wasn't something the researchers expected to find. These driven leaders were self-effacing and modest. They consistently pointed to the contribution of others and didn't like drawing attention to themselves. The good to great leaders never wanted to become larger-than-life heroes. Collis writes, "They never aspired to be put on a pedestal or become unreachable icons. They were seemingly ordinary people quietly producing extraordinary results."

When Collins interviewed people who worked for these leaders, he said they "continually used words like quiet, humble, modest, served, shy, gracious, mild-mannered, self-effacing, understated." Collins didn't believe his own chipping and so forth to describe them.

Here it appears it is the open acknowledgment of humility that is valuable. There is recognition that humility works, that it goes far in building respect for those who have it and inspires trust and confidence from people around them.

Yes, astoundingly, humility sometimes attracts the world's notice.

"For all these things my hand has made, and so all these things have come into being (by and for Me), says the Lord, but this is the man to whom I look and have regard; he who is humble and of a broken and wounded spirit, and who trembles at my word revers my commands" (Isa. 66:2, AMP).

This profound passage points us to an altogether different motivation and purpose for humility than we will ever find in the pages of a secular business manual. Here we find motivation and purpose rooted in this amazing fact, humility draws the gaze of our Sovereign God.

If we understand the background of the passage, we find even richer meaning. Here God is addressing the Israelites, a people with a unique identity, chosen by God from all the Torah—the law of God—but they didn't tremble at this word. In a sense, they had everything going except what was most important. They lacked humility before God.

So in this passage, God in his mercy drawing the Israelite's attention away from their prideful assumption of privilege as his chosen people and away from their preoccupation with the trapping of religions.

These things don't attract his active and gracious gaze, but humility does.

Men of power are men of humility, and men of humility are men of power. Humility is the doorway to power from on high.

So What Is Humility?

Our definition of humility must be biblical and not simply pragmatic, and in order to be biblical, it must begin with God. As John Calvin wrote, "It is evident that man never attain to am true self-knowledge until he has previously contemplated the face of God, and come down after such contemplation to look into himself."

Humility is honestly assessing ourselves in the right of God's holiness and our sinfulness. Genuine humility is knowing you are nothing and you are all because of the Lord Jesus Christ.

In our pursuit to fulfill God's end-time agenda and purpose, we should be driven by the amazing promise humility holds out to us. God gives grace to the humble! In our ventures, we must be aware of the need for God's grace to give efforts. The lasting value of God's providential power is embedded in humility.

The sad fact is that none of us are immune to the logic-defying, blinding effects of pride. Though it shows up in many and to a differing degree, it impacts us all. The real issue here is not if pride exists and how pride is being expressed in your heart, it's where pride exists and how pride is being expressed in your life. Scripture shows us that pride is strongly and dangerously rooted in all our lives far more than most of us come to admit or even think about it.

At every stage of our Christian development and at every stage of our Christian discipleship, pride is the greatest enemy and humility is our greatest friend.

Throughout our time on this earth and in every arena of our lives, you and I share a common greatest enemy, which is pride. Pride has quite the history, one that precedes humanity.

Pride, it seems, was the very first sin, according to Isaiah 14 records the downfall of a king but not a mere earthly ruler. This king is the embodiment of God-defying arrogance, but the language used here apparently references the rebellion and fall of Satan himself. Isaiah 14:13, the motivation behind Satan's rebellion is exposed, "You said in your heart, I will ascend to heaven, and above the stars of God I will set my throne on high." It was led by the prideful Lucifer's powerful angelic creatures possessing beauty and glory far beyond our comprehension. They arrogantly desired recognition and status equal to God Himself. In response, God swiftly and severely judged them.

Pride is not only the earliest but it is at the core of all sin. "Pride", John Stott wrote, "is more than the first of the seven deadly sins, it is itself the essence of all sin."

Indeed, from God's perspective, pride seems to be the most serious sin. From my careful study, I'm convinced beyond every reasonable doubt that there's nothing God hates more than this. God righteously hates all sins, of course, but biblical evidence abounds for the conclusion that there's no son more offensive to him than pride.

When his word reveals those things "that the Lord hates" and "that are an abomination to him" "It's the proud man's haughty eyes" that head up the list in Proverbs 8:13 (NIV).

Consider the divine perspective on pride revealed in Proverbs 16:5, "Everyone who is arrogant in heart is an abomination to the Lord, be assured, he will not go unpunished."

When No One Acclaims
What's God's

Why does God hate pride so passionately? Here's why, when one begins to feel self-sufficient independent of God. Pride is when sinful human being aspires to the status and positing of God the creator and refuse to acknowledge their dependency upon him.

Charles Bridge once noted how pride lifts up one's heart against God and "contends for supremacy" with him. That's a keenly insightful and biblical definition of pride's essence—contending for supremacy with God and lifting up our hearts against him.

Pride takes numerable forms but has only one end, self-glorification. That's the motive and ultimate purpose of pride, to rob God of legitimate glory and to pursue pride, self-glorification, contending for supremacy with him. The proud person seeks to glorify himself and not God, thereby attempting in effect to do deprive God of something only he is worthy to receive.

The end-time army accolades or praise that belongs to the almighty. That is why the end-time army is clothed in humility and showed in soberness in Christ.

God opposes pride and it's no wonder why he hates pride. Let's be careful of pride; pride is a cancer that kills fast. John Calvin wrote, "God cannot bear with seeing his glory appreciated by the creature in even the smallest degree, so intolerable to him is the sacrilegious arrogance of those who, by praising themselves, obscure his glory as far as they can."

And because God cannot tolerate or bear with this arrogance, he reveals himself in scripture as actively opposed to pride as an immediate and constant activity. The proud will not indefinitely escape discipline.

Jonathan Edwards called pride "the worse viper that is in the heart" and "the greatest disturber of the soul's peace and sweet communion with Christ." He ranked pride as the most difficult sin to root and "the most hidden, secret and deceitful of all lust."

C. J. Mahaney said, "By unmasking pride as well as introducing us to humility our greatest friend, God is laying out for us the path to true greatness, a path that we will see most clearly in our Savior's Life and Death."

One of the deadliest things any human can do is to ascribe glory to self when is supposed to be going to God.

As a pastor, people come to me after service, and sometimes people mail letters to me, telling me how my messages and teachings have transformed them, healed them, and delivered them from obscurity and challenges of life, but that is the things they are thanking me. I know I have no power to do all the things; there are things to thank for, but that is the thinking me for and so instead of the glory coming to he me. I internationally transfer the glory of God because ministering to these people is a privilege that comes from God that I don't deserve, so as I thank them for their kinds words, I quietly transfer the glory to God.

Yes, leaders are vital to the church, and it's appropriate to thank those leaders who have been used by God as a man as of his grace. However, we're to ascribe glory to no man. "Glory is ascribed exclusively and entirely to God. Only he can regenerate a heart. Only he can change life; therefore, only God should receive glory."

Whatever successes we experienced in our life and ministry and vocation, learn how to immediately transfer the glory to him.

If your business is successful, are you transferring the glory for that success to him? If people compliment you for your effective parenting, do you transfer to glory to him? Recognize that though you're a means of grace to your children, you can't in and of yourself transform your children; only God can, and as He does, only He gets the glory.

The Holy Spirit is training us in humility to rule and reign with Jesus as His bride. If we are to be yoked to the bridge groom, we must wear the same wedding garments he wore.

Jesus the king of kings chose a crown of thorns. How many more should we adorn ourselves in the beauty of meekness! He forsook his divine robes of righteousness for earthly homes and robes. How many more should we cover ourselves with a mental of humility?

At the marriage supper of the Lamb, each one of us will be wrapped in brilliant garments reflecting the fruits and rewards of our earthly lives. Stunning, tailor-made royal robes will be our portion. During our time on earth, however, it is all of our outer garments. They are simple burlap robes. Underneath are the beautiful fabrics of our gifting. Sometimes the Lord displays these openly, but generally they remain a secret testimony between him and us.

The goal is to be so accepted and confident in the light of the world that we do not need the limelight. At the end of the day, His opinion is the only one that counts! When we are rooted and grounded in his affections, it is easier not to care about promoting ourselves. It is then that we find ourselves in that wonderful place of reckless abandonment of being a true lover of Jesus.

R. C. Sproul wrote, "The grand difference between a human being and a supreme being is precisely this: Apart from God, I cannot exist. Apart from me, God does exist. God does not me in order for him to be; I do not need God in order for me to be. That is the difference between what we call self-existent being and dependent being. We are dependent, we are fragile. We cannot live without air, without water, without food.

No human being has the power of being within needs support system from birth to death to sustain life. We are like flowers that bloom and then wither and then fade. This is how we differ from God. God does not wither, God does not fade, and God is not fragile."

Matthew Henry expressed it this way, "The greatest and best man in the world must say, by the grace of God. I am what I am, but God says absolutely . . . I am that I am."

As we investigate such attributes, we become increasingly and indescribably aware of the vast distance between ourselves and God.

Ironically, this distance from God will be even more real to us when we got closer to God in heaven as Jonathan Edwards reminds us, "The Saints in Glory are so much employed in praise, because they are perfect in humility, and have so great a sense of the infinite distance between them and God."

Even now the more you're aware of this distance and this difference between you and God, the more you will experience and express humility, and you'll say with experience and express humility and you'll say with David, "Such knowledge is too wonderful to me; it is high; I cannot attain it" (Ps. 139:6).

"Whatever exalts himself will be humbled, and whoever humbles himself will be exalted" (Matt. 23:12, NIV).

Humble yourself, is an active verb, the point I want to make here is that humility is a matter of personal choice. Are you humble? If you are, it is because you have decided that you will be humble. If you are not, it is because you have not decided to be humble. I realize that what I have just said may sound simplistic, but the Bible refers to humble yourself, and that is a very simple language. It is an active verb.

You don't pay for humility, you live it, you don't pray for humility, and you do humility, which means that humility has to be attained.

Jesus Teaching Humility

Jesus taught extensively on humility during his earthly ministry, and he also exemplified the true essence of humility. In fact he is an embodiment of humility and what it means.

"After he was found in (term of his) outward appearance as a man (for a divinely-appointed time), he bumbled himself (still further) by becoming obedient (to the Father) to the point of death, even death on a cross." (Phil. 2:8, AMP).

The Bible declares, "Let this mind be in you, which was also in Christ Jesus" (Phil. 2:5).

What does "this mind" refer to? "Jesus humbled Himself" (Phil. 2:8). Even though he was God, he agreed to take on and live His life on earth through a human nature even going so far as to die a human death on the cross. Humility was at the core of Jesus's life and ministry, and we must have this same mindset if we are going to be everything that God wants us to be.

"Blessed are the poor in spirit, for there is in the kingdom of heaven . . . Blessed are the meek, humbles, for they shall inherit the earth" (Matt. 5:3–5).

"Learn from me, For I am gentle (meek, humble, and lowly in heart, and you will find rest for your souls)" (Matt. 11:29).

"Whoever humbles himself as this little child is the greatest in the Kingdom of Heaven" (Matt. 18:4).

"Whoever desire to become great among you, let him be your servant and whosever desire to be first among you, let him be your slave" (Matt. 20:26–27).

True humility is in service and true greatness is in humility. Until you are humble and serve, you are not yet great, or to feel great is when people serve you. They are at your beck and call but are wrong. It is when you don't think highly of yourself and you become a servant, that is when you become great.

"He who is greatest among you shall be your Servant" (Luke 14:11).

"Everyone who exalts himself will be humbled, and he who humbles himself will be exalted" (Luke 18:14).

"If I then, your Lord and Teacher, have washed your feet, you are also ought to wash one another's feet (John 13:14).

"He who is greatest among you, let him be as the younger and he who governs as he who serves…I am among you as the one who serves" (Luke 22:26–27).

So What Does Humility Looks Like

It is important to recognize true humility when you see it. Nothing helps more to recognize true humility than to know what phony or counterfeit humility looks like.

The most effective and ordacions way to begin the process of comprehending true humility is to take a close look at the life of a person that the Bible characterizes as humble. I have found it helpful in this regard to look to Moses as a good example of humbleness.

The Humility of Moses

Moses is one of my outstanding biblical personalities, and he is highly regarded as such by all.

He has also gone down in history as one of the outstanding leaders of the human race. Very few people would deny Moses that distinction and honor. He was a powerful leader and an incomparable role model for people of all religions. Yet according to Number 12:3, "The man Moses was very humble more than all men who were on the face of the earth."

This typifies that Moses was the humblest man on the planet at that time. Some Bible translators use the word meekest instead of humblest to render the Hebrew language. So in Moses, we have a combination of the most powerful leader in all the world leaders and the humblest individual. This fits well with what Jesus would say centuries later. "He who humbles himself will be exalted" (Matt. 23:12).

Miriam Exalted Herself

In Numbers 12, Moses's' sister Miriam suddenly wanted to replace Moses as the leader of the children of Israel. She recruited Aaron and attempted a coup. Moses, however, rose to the occasion and endured the attacks and criticism with dignity and integrity. It was a serious enough matter to cause God to intervene personally. He told Miriam and Aaron directly that Moses was his appointed and anointed leader. Miriam had exalted herself, and God, true to his nature, responded by humbling her. He punished Miriam, apparently the ring leader of the rebellion, with an instant case of leprosy. Moses again showed his true character when he prayed for Miriam to be healed. God, as we know, miraculously healed her. However, while Miriam had been restored, she was never the same. The only notation we read about Miriam after that incident was that she died and that she was buried (Num. 20:1).

Anytime God has to step in and humble you, it means it is too late! It is much better to humble yourself as a part of your ongoing lifestyle following the examples of Moses.

Please Understand This Humility

Jesus said, "I am gentle and lowly in heart" (Matt. 11:29). The word gentle in the New King James Version is translated meek in some other versions. It is related to the Greek word *prayotes*. In fact, the New Living Translation renders the statement, "I am humble and gentle." Jesus, I realize, is the second person of _____ and thus God Himself, but we can still follow his lead. We should also be able to say, "I am humble and gentle," especially since both characteristics are listed in Galatians 5 as a fruit of the Holy Spirit.

Paul, however, was a human being just as we are. In 2 Corinthians, the epistle in which he most assuredly displayed his credentials as an apostle, Paul also wrote, "I, Paul, myself am pleading with you by the meekness and gentleness of Christ who in presence am lowly along you" (2 Cor. 10:1).

The word meekness that is used here also comes from the Greek word *prayotes* the word for humility. Paul apparently had no problem in personally identifying with Jesus's assertion that he was humble. Therefore, while Paul was exalted by God as an apostle, he also recognized that one reason that Lord God had seen fit to do this was because he (Paul) had chosen to be humble himself.

Humility Is Not Dress Code

We have this legalistic mentality that modest dressing or a specific way of dressing exemplifies humility, which is not true. Some people decided that their rules will involve a dress code. They reason that people will see that they are humble if they do not wear makeup or jewelry. My sign of humility is preaching in jeans and an open shirt instead of a tie and a shirt and a suit. I let my beard grow without trimming it, and I hardly ever comb my hair. I do not believe in buying expensive clothes or in keeping up with the latest fashions.

Legalism can apply to other lifestyle issues, too. My house is more modest than the lavish one that you live in. Look! I have an older model car than you. You live in a gated community? What kind of a testimony is that I live in an integrated neighborhood and most of my neighbors belong to nonwhite ethnic groups?

So What Is Not Humility

Many other subtle and equality deceptive often parade as signs of humility. A Christian writer John Bevere, for example, quotes the apostle Paul saying, "For I am the least of the Apostle, who am not worthy to be called an Apostle" (1 Cor. 15:9). Bevere's comment was "Counterfeit humility knows how to be used politically correct words in order to appear humble, yet there is no loveliness of heart or mind." This is a real danger that the last days' army should never fall into it. We must be conscious. But he adds, "When Paul said he was the bottom of the barrel of the apostle, it wasn't politically correct jargon but rather true humility." Here is a distinction that we would do well to keep in mind. False humility may take on forms other than legalism provides a helpful distinction.

Other common badges of counterfeit or phony humility might include being proof, belittling yourself, being chronically ill, being weak, atoning others to walk all over you. Seeing yourself as a worm as the line in Charles Wesley's hymn: "Such a worm as I." Although Wesley himself did not lead word theology and has a doormat mentality, shy, I have noticed that some misdirected authors apparently think it is humble not to include a byline on their manuscripts or articles.

The dictionary defines humbleness as "not proud or arrogant, modest, to be humble although successful." This is what we really should aim for.

Humility Does Not
Mean Perfection

The recognition and admission of being humble do not mean we are perfect. God requires us to be humble just as he requires us to be holy, but He has never required or even expected us to be perfect. Some people have not understood this important distinction because they remember what Jesus said, "Therefore you shall be perfect, just as your Father in heaven is perfect" (Matt. 5:48). This is a classic translation problem. Perfect in this verse comes from the Greek *teleios*. The meaning of *teleios* is not a flawless moral nature but maturity. He has required or even expected, us to be perfect, but what Jesus was saying is that we are supposed to live up to everything that God wants us to be.

The problem is that almost all English translations render teleios as perfect and that can only throw us offtrack at this point. The only translation I found that really brings out the meaning is Eugene Peterson's The Message, which declares, "In a words, what I am saying is, Grow up. You're kingdom subjects. Now live like it. Live out your God-created identity. Live generously and graciously toward others, the way God lives toward you." Once we understand that this, we know how we can be humble without the same time being perfect.

We should not, therefore, think of humility or being humble as absolutes. It is not that you are either humble as absolute. It is not that you are either humble or you are not. Humility is not absolute.

Humility is not similar to being pregnant. We cannot say that one pregnant woman is more pregnant than another. Humility, on the other hand, is a range. Not all humble people are equal. They are none like the National Football League quarterbacks. There are dozens of quarterbacks in the NFL, and every single one of them is a good quarterback or they would not be where they are, but they are not all equal. Some are better quarterbacks than others.

Growing in humility is a lifelong process. I pray that the Almighty will help this last generation army to grow in this humility.

"Therefore, lay aside all filthiness and overflow of wickedness and receive with meekness is the implanted word, which is able to save your souls" (James 1:21).

C. Peter Wagner, chancellor of the Wagner Leadership Institute and president of Global Harvest Ministries in his book *Humility* said to be humble or not to be humble is a choice each of us makes. I base this blunt thought on the foundational scripture for this chapter. "Whoever exalts himself will be humbled and he who humbles himself will be exalted" (Matt. 23:12). This quote from Jesus is built around action words. What you finally achieve in your Life will clearly depend on the decisions, you make now, and the actions you take to implement those decisions. Jesus would not have put you in this way unless he knew that you had the power to humble yourself or to exalt yourself.

The way you make this decision, has to do with the way you think essentially,

And be not conformed to this world; but be ye transformed by the renewing of your mind, that ye may prove what that good, and acceptable and perfect will is.

For I say, through the grace given unto me, to every man that is among you not to think of yourself more higher than you he ought to think; but to think soberly, according as God has dealt to every man the measure of faith. (Rom. 12:2–3)

There are two operative phrases in this scripture, one in each verse:

Verse 2: "The renewing of your mind." If we renew our minds, we can be transformed. This frees us to do God's will. Renewing our minds has to do with how we think. This not a matter of our hearts. It is a matter of our minds.

Verse 3: "Think soberly of yourself." This means that we are supposed to be very clear in our own self-perception as to exactly who God has created each of us to be. We are not random happenstance on this earth. God has designed each of us for a specific purpose, and He desires to fulfill His purpose.

King Josiah made a decision to humble himself. Josiah, an example of humility, makes us understand how humility enables a person to reach his or her potential. When Josiah became a king, idolatry had penetrated every stratum of society in Judah. Josiah did the right thing and he inquired to the Lord. He discovered through the prophet Huldah that God has decided to "bring calamity on this place and its inhabits" (2 King 22:16) because they were worshipping other gods, But the Lord also told Josiah that he would have peace during his own reign. The Lord said, "Your eyes shall not see all the calamity which I will bring on this place" (2 Kings 22:19). That is high as you can go in fulfilling God's purpose for your life! He ended up exalted because he was humble. Uzziah, like Josiah, was one of the kings of Judah who belonged to the select group of those who "did what was right in the sight of the Lord" (2 Chron. 26:4). God honored Uzziah's faith by making him an awesome warrior whose "fame spread as far as the entrance of Egypt, for he became exceedingly strong" (2 Chron. 26:8). He was a good man and one of the greatest heroes of his generation.

But Uzziah made a huge mistake by deciding to exalt himself. When he was strong his heart was lifted up to his destruction" (2 Chron. 26:16). How did he do it? In those days, only the priest was allowed to go into the temple and burn incense to the Lord, but Uzziah decided that if the priest could do it, so could he. Since he was a great king, he decided that he did not have to humble himself and admit that the priest could do something that he could not do. So Uzziah, against the warning of the priests, made the bad decision to go into the sanctuary and burn incense. What were the results?

God had to step in and humble the king. What was the result? God had to step in and humble the king. God struck him with leprosy. And while he was still king, he was forced to live isolated in quarantine for the rest of his life!

William Branham

A huge wave of change swept into the church after World War II. But back in the late 1940s and early 1950s, the wall between evangelicals and Pentecostals was so high that the Holy Spirit has to speak separately to both sectors. The two who became best known for hearing what the spirit was saying and taking leadership of the new movement of evangelism were Billy Graham and William Branham of the Pentecostals.

When we recently moved into the twenty-first century, numerous periodicals published hits of the most influential people of the preceding century. Billy Graham's name was on virtually every list. But William Branham's name wasn't anywhere. William who? Today, only a few well-informed old-timers can tell you who Branham was. He was all but forgotten.

This is very odd because for two decades, week by week, meeting by meeting. Branham's meetings were much larger than Graham's.

Branham would deliver prophecies and seemingly at will. He would, with pinpoint accuracy, call out people's names, family members, social security numbers, and other private information. After his meetings, there would be huge piles of crutches and rows of empty wheelchairs left by people who had been healed—something unseen at Billy Graham's meetings. Message for a message, many more people found the road to heaven through Branham than through Graham. But now we ask, "William who?" What happened?

I am indebted to research done by Eddie Hyatt for the answer to this crucial question before I quote from him; however, it is important to know that Gordon Lindsay is an important player in the story. Lindsay was the editor of *The Voice of Healing* magazine. (He later founded Christ for the Nations Institute in Dallas, Texas, to this day one of the finest schools in the world for Christian leaders. He is deceased but his widow Freda carries on strongly.) As this story unfolds, Lindsey was serving as the campaign manager for William Branham.

Here are some extremely revealing paragraphs from Eddie Hyatt's research:

When the time came for Branham to preach the evening services, Lindsay would introduce him in a low-key manner while at the same time acknowledging that God was using him in a remarkable way. Once, when Lindsay was away, a brother B introduced Branham. His flowery introduction was filled with glowing accolades and referred to Branham as a special end-time prophet of God. When Lindsay returned, Branham said, "Brother Lindsay, I would like Brother B to introduce me from now on."

Branham then began to surround himself with individuals who fed his ego with ideas about being a special end-time prophet of God. Lindsay fought to warn him, but his advice was not heeded and later withdrew from involvement in Branham's ministry.

This was the beginning of a sad departure from the simple humility in which Branham had begun. He eventually came to believe that he was the fulfillment of the promise of God in Malachi 4:5 which says, "I will send Elijah the prophet before the coming of the great and dreadful day of the Lord." Branham believed that in the same way, John the Baptist fulfilled this scripture before the first coming of Christ, that he was the fulfillment of the same scripture before the second coming of Christ. He believed that he was in reality Elijah preparing the way for the coming of Christ.

William Branham was a good man like Uzziah. He started in humility and God exalted him. But God's exaltation was not enough. Branham made the unwise decision to exalt himself, and he arrived at that point where God has to step in and humble him. In this case, it was definitely too late for Branham. Here is what happened:

In 1965, Lindsay received a call from out of state asking him to come and pray for Branham who had been in a car accident and was in serious condition. Because of his previous experience, Lindsay felt that he was to leave the situation completely in the hands of God, and so he did not go. Branham died shortly thereafter, and it was reported that his head was swollen twice its normal size from the injuries of the impact.

The Garment of Humility

There are different kinds of garments. There is a garment of righteousness, there is a garment of power, and there is also a garment of joy and praise. "To appoint unto them that mourn in Zion, to give unto them beauty for ashes, the oil of joy for mourning, the garment of praise for the spirit of heaviness, that they might be called trees of righteousness, the planting of the Lord, that might be glorified" (Isa. 61:3).

The Holy Spirit is training us in humility to rule and reign with Jesus as His Bride. If we are to be yoked to the bridegroom, we must wear the same wedding garments He wore. Jesus, the king of kings, chose a crown of thorns. How much more should we adorn ourselves in the beauty of meekness? He forsook His divine robes of righteousness for earthly homespun robes. How much more should we color ourselves with a mantle of humility?

At the Marriage Supper of the Lamb, each one of us will be wrapped in brilliant garments reflecting the prints and rewards of our earthly lives. Stunning, tailor-made royal robes will be our portion. During our time on earth, however, it is as if our outer garments are simple burlap robes. Underneath are the beautiful fabrics of our gifting. Sometimes the Lord displays these openly, but generally they remain a secret testimony between Him and us.

The goal is to be accepted and confident in the light of the world that we do not need the limelight. At the end of the day, His opinion is the only one that counts. When we are rooted and grounded in His affections, it is easier not to care about promoting ourselves. It is then that we find ourselves in that wonderful place of reckless abandonment of being a true lover of Jesus.

This Generation Will Not Conform

This generation, I mean the end-time army, has a double responsibility in relation to the world around us. On the other hand, we are to live, serve, and witness in the world. On the other hand, we are to avoid becoming contaminated by the world. So we neither seek to preserve our holiness by escaping from the world or sacrifice our holiness by conforming to the world. Escapism and conformism are thus both forbidden to us. God is calling out a people for himself and is summoning us to be different from everybody else. "Be holy," He says repeatedly to his people, "because I am holy" (e.g., Lev. 11:45; 1 Pet. 1:15–16). This foundational theme recurs in all four of the main sections of scripture: the law, the prophets, the teaching of Jesus, and the teaching of the apostles.

First, the law God sends to his people through Moses. "You must not do as they do in the Land of Canaan, where I am bringing you.

Do not follow their practices. You must obey my laws and be careful to follow my decrees. I am the Lord your God." (Lev. 18:3–4). Similarly, God's criticism of his people through the prophet Ezekiel is that "you have not followed my decrees or kept my laws but have conformed to the standards of the nations around you" (Ezek. 11:12). It is the same in the New Testament. In the Sermon on the Mount, Jesus spoke of the hypocrites and the pagans and added, "Do not be like them" (Matt. 6:8). Finally, the apostle Paul wrote to the Romans, "Do not conform to the pattern of this world, but be transformed by the renewing of your mind" (Rom. 12:2).

Here then is God's call to radical discipleship to radical nonconformity to the surrounding culture. It is a call to develop a Christian counter-culture, a call to engagement without compromise. So what are the contemporary trends which threaten to swallow us up in which we must resist?

The Pluralism

Pluralism affirms that every *ism* has its own independent validity and an equal right to our respect. It, therefore, rejects Christian claims to finality and uniqueness and condemns us as sheer arrogance the attempt to convert anybody (let alone everybody) to what it sees as merely our own opinions.

How should we respond to the spirit of pluralism? It should be with great humility, I hope, and with no hint of personal superiority. But we must continue to affirm the uniqueness and the finality of Jesus Christ for he is unique in his incarnation (the one and only God-man), unique in his atonement (only he has died for the sins of the world), and unique in his resurrection (only he has conquered death). And since in no other person but Jesus of Nazareth did God first become human (in his birth) then bear our sins in his death and then triumph over death (in his resurrection), he is uniquely competent to save sinners. Nobody else possesses his qualifications. So we may talk about Alexander the

Great, Charles the Great, and Napoleon Bonaparte but not Jesus the Great. He is not *the great*; he is the only. There is nobody like him. He has no rival and no successor.

A second widespread secular trend that Christian disciples have to resist is that of materialism. Materialism is not simply an acceptance of the reality of the material world. If that were the case, all Christians would be materialistic since we believe that God has created the material world and made its blessings available to us. God has also affirmed the material order through the incarnation and resurrection of his son in the water of baptism and the bread and wine in holy communion. It is no wonder that William Temple described Christianity as the most material of all religions. But it is not materialistic.

Materialism—a preoccupation with material things—can smother our spiritual life. Jesus told us not to store up treasure on earth and warned us against covetousness. So did the apostle Paul, urging us instead to develop a lifestyle of simplicity, generosity, and contentment, drawing on his own experience of having learned to be content in whatever circumstances he was (Phil. 4:11).

Paul added that "godliness with contentment is great gain" (1 Tim. 6:6) and then went on to explain that "we brought nothing into the world, and we can take nothing out of it." Perhaps he was consciously echoing Job who said, "Naked I came from my mother's womb, and naked I will depart" (Job 1:21). In other words, life on earth is a brief pilgrimage between two moments of nakedness. So we would be wise to travel light. We shall take nothing will us.

Dealing with Narcissism

In Greek mythology, Narcissus was a handsome young man who caught sight of his reflection in a pond, fell in love with his own image, toppled into the water, and drowned. So narcissism is an excessive love for oneself and unbounded admiration of self. In the 1970s narcissism found expression in the Human Potential movement, which laid emphasis on the need for self-actualization.

In the 19080s and 1990s the New Age movement jumped on the bandwagon of the Human Potential Movement. Shirley MacLaine could be called its high priestess, and she was infatuated with herself. According to her good news goes like this, "I know that I exist; therefore I am, I know the god force exists; therefore it is since I am a part of that force, I am that I am."

It sounds like a deliberate parody of God's revelation of himself to Moses, "I AM who I AM" (Exod. 3:14).

The New Age Movement calls us to look inside ourselves, to explore ourselves for the solutions to our problems are within. We do not need a savior to come to us from somewhere else; we can be our own savior. Unfortunately, some of this teaching has permeated the church with some Christians urging that we must not only love God and our neighbor, but we must also love ourselves. But no, this is surely a mistake for three reasons. First, Jesus spoke of "the first and great commandment" and of the second but did not mention a third. Secondly, self-love is one of the signs of the last days (2 Tim. 3:2). Thirdly, the meaning of agape love is the sacrifice of oneself in the service of oneself is clearly nonsense!

What then should our attitude be to ourselves? It is a combination of self-affirmation and self-denial—affirmation of everything in us that comes from our creation and redemption and denying everything that can be traced to the fall.

It is a great relief to turn away from an unhealthy preoccupation with oneself to the healthy commandments of God, united and reinforced by Jesus to love God with our whole being and to love our neighbor as ourselves. For God intends his church to be a community of love, a worshipping and serving community.

Everybody knows that love is the greatest thing in the world and believers know why. It is because God is love. The thirteenth-century Spanish courtier, Raymond Lull (a missionary to Muslims in North

Africa) wrote that "he who loves not, lives not." For living is loving and without love, the human personality disintegrates. That is why everybody is looking for an authentic relationship of love.

We have configured four major secular trends that threaten to engulf the Christian community.

We are not to be like reeds shaken by the wind, bowing down before the guests of public opinion but unmovable like rocks in a mountain stream. We are not to be like fish floating with the stream (for "only dead fish swim with the current" as Malcolm Muggeridge put it) but to swim against the stream even against the cultural mainstream. We are not to be like chameleons, lizards that change according to their surroundings but to stand out visibly against our surroundings.

What then are Christians to be like if we are not to be like reeds, dead fish, or chameleons? Is God's word entirely negative, simply telling us to avoid being molded into the shape of those around us? No, it is positive. We are to be like Christ, "conformed to the image of God's son" (Rom. 8:29).

John Scott, one of the finest teachers and communicators of scriptures in his unmatchable book *The Radical Disciple*, said, "To be mature is to have a mature relationship with Christ in which we worship, trust, love and obey him." And I agree absolutely because that is the only way to bring us to that place where we realize we are nothing without Him, and whatever we are is because of Him. And that keeps us humble and noble. If you desire to know or learn anything to your advantage, then take delight in being unknown and unregarded.

A true understanding and humble estimate of oneself is the highest and most valuable of all lessons. To take no account of one's self, but always to think well and highly of others is the highest wisdom and perfection! Should you see another person openly doing evil or carrying out a wicked purpose, do not on that account consider yourself better than him for you cannot tell how long you will remain in a state of grace. We are all frail, consider none frailer than yourself. If it seems to you that you know a great deal and have wide experience in many fields, yet remember that there are matters of which you are ignorant, so do not be conceited but confess your ignorance. Why do you wish to esteem yourself above others when there are many who are wiser and more perfect in the law of God?

Everyone naturally defies knowledge, but of what use is the knowledge itself without the fear of God? A humble countryman who serves God is more pleasing to Him than a conceited intellectual who knows the lives of the stars but neglects his own soul. A man who truly knows himself realizes his own worthlessness and takes no pleasure in the praises of men. We are absolutely nothing without Jesus. The rising army of the last days knows that they are unmovable without him. They are powerless without him. Thank you, Jesus, for counting this last days' army worthy for the end-time commission and mandate.

Supernatural Generation

We have seen miracles, signs, healing, and wonders. Some of us have read them from the Bible and church history. Some of us also have heard and we have been told, but everything we have read, seen, and told is nowhere comparable to what God is doing with this undercover generation, the last days' army. It has no precedent; the world has never seen anything like this before. Words cannot describe and the human mind and intellect cannot apprehend; it has never happened before, neither has it been experienced before. I am talking about raw power—supernatural, mind-blowing, and mind-boggling miracles, revival, signs, and wonders and healing, creative and recreative miracles, special and notable miracles.

"Eye has not seen, nor ear heard, nor have entered into the heart of man, the things which God has prepared for those who love Him" (1 Cor. 2:9).

"Do not remember the former things, nor consider the things of old. Behold I will do a new thing, Now it shall bring forth, shall you not know it? I will even make a road in the wilderness and rivers in the desert" (Isa. 43:18–19).

We have read in the book of Acts on the day of Pentecost how the Holy Spirit came upon them mightily.

"And when the day of Pentecost was fully come, they were all with one accord in one place. And suddenly there came a sound from heaven as of a rushing might wind, and it filled all the house where they were sitting. And there appeared unto them cloven tongues like as of fire, and it sat upon each of them. And they were all filled with the Holy Ghost and began to speak with other tongues, as the Spirit gave them utterance" (Acts 2:1–4).

By these Holy Spirit empowerment, the early church moved in the supernatural signs and wonders. Peter spoke and three thousand people gave their lives to Christ in one meeting. In Acts 3:1–11, Peter, James, and John were going into the temple to pray at the ninth hour, and they saw a lame man who had been lame from birth and sat at the gate of the temple begging for alms, and Peter commanded the lame man to walk, and he took him by the hand and he started walking. The Bible says the people were filled with wonder and amazement at that which has happened unto him.

We also read in the book of Acts how Peter's shadow healed the sick.

"In so much that they brought forth the sick into the streets and laid them on the beds and couches, that at the least the shadow of Peter passing by might over shadow some of them" (Act 5:15).

"Crowds also gathered from the towns around Jerusalem, bringing the sick and those tormented by unclean spirit, and all of them were healed" (Acts 5:16).

Paul the apostle also did mighty works of God. He raised the dead and it was also said of him, "And God worked special miracles by the hands of Paul, so that even handkerchiefs and aprons that had touched him were taken to the sick, and the disease and evil spirits left them" (Acts 19:11–12).

These are just but a few of what God did with the early church's apostles. Within fifty years, the early church read the Gospel of Jesus Christ globally. They published it everywhere in the world; that is the New Testament. Now let's go back to the Old Testament. We saw the mighty acts of God through His servant Moses, how he parted the Red Sea into two and the Israelites crossed over to the other side, how he turned the Nile River into blood, and let down his rod. It turned into a snake and swallowed up the pharaoh's magicians' snakes and picked it by the tail, and it turned back into a rod. We also read Elijah prayed and fire came down from heaven. He also shut the heavens and there was no rain, and he prayed for rain after a long drought which he had caused. And there was rain, raised the dead, miraculously multiplied food, and brought reformation to a backslidden people.

The last days' army, the undercover generation, will have power over nature and command fire to come down.

"These have power to shut heaven, that it rain in the days of their prophecy; and have power over waters to turn them blood and smite the earth with all plagues, as often as they will" (Rev. 11:6).

They will have authority over the four elements of nature—sea, earth, sky, and wind, fire. They will come out of their mouths when they speak. They will do unimaginable, great exploits, unpredicted. The last days' army will operate and will walk in the powers of the age to come. They will do great and awesome wonders and the miracles that they will do will have no precedent in the history book, in church history, and even in the Bible. We cannot even imagine or visualize how it will be.

This last days' army will experience the supernatural in dimensions we have never experienced before. They will experience a supernatural transformation of what I call translocation or tele-transportation where you are carried and transported bodily by the Holy Spirit to different places on the earth. Elijah was commonly transported supernaturally by the Holy Spirit, and it was common knowledge to all people that he was frequently carried by the spirit.

"And it shall come to pass, as soon as I am gone from thee, that the Spirit of the Lord shall carry thee whither I know not, and so when I come and tell Ahab, and he cannot find thee, be shall slay me; but they servant fear the Lord from my youth" (1 King 18:12).

The last days' army will operate in the supernatural frequency of the spirit in such a way that they will defile nature laws. They will stop the sun from going down, they will defy the law of gravity, and they will throw the law of physics into oblivion. There is coming glory revival that the church has never witnessed and experienced before. Watch out! There is going to be an unusual increase in the supernatural, great explosions of the power of God. There is going to be such glory that the church has never heard, read, or witnessed before. It is a combination of former and the latter glory being poured upon this last days' army.

"Ask ye of the Lord rain in the time of the latter rain, so the Lord shall make bright clouds, and give them showers of rain, to every one grass in the field" (Zach. 10:1).

"The glory of this latter house shall be greater than of the former, saith the Lord of hosts: and in this place will I give peace, saith the Lord of hosts" (Hag. 2:9).

The presence and the glory of God in these last days shall be so intense that the church which is the body of Christ will come together in true worship in spirit and truth and bask in the awe of God's presence, and the multitude shall come to the brightness of His shining.

We have seen remarkable power in the past in the Bible and church's history, but all of that is just a "previous to the coming attractions" of what is about to take place in those last days. In fact, the supernatural that we have read and seen and experienced in the past will all pale in comparison to the outpouring of this new power and glory that God is outpouring on the last days away. There will be tangible glory of the power of God, evidence with supernatural satisfaction. Limbs will grow out and today parts will be recreated right in front of the masses. The climate will be a glorious atmosphere. It will be heaven on earth.

There is an entire refined, supernatural generation of sons and daughters who will beam forth with more radiance than any other generation. They will mold a powerful kingdom, dynamic; they are carriers of revival fire and operate in new dimensions of God's glory yet to be witnessed.

They will be transformed in their thinking about the power of God that signs, wonders, and miracles will become common occurrences, a supernatural part of life. God's spirit is moving so powerfully that there is unusual shifting in the atmosphere. What God is doing in these last days with the last days coming is so supernatural that the paradigm of the yesterdays can no longer apply to today.

The undercover generation will take the kingdom's territory. They will turn nations, cities, and continents upside down for Jesus. It is a drastic change. It's a crossover of thoughts, transformations of natural thought to spiritual thought, a coming out of an old kinsman and into a new form from a physical realm into a spiritual one.

Are you ready to be a sign and a wonder that topple the natural earthly order of things and contradict the law of physics? By your command, hurricanes will stop and have them obey if you walk in the laws of the spirit.

The undercover generation will shift into the higher law of the spirit to render the physical law inoperative. When we do, God may just release us as a sign to answer the spiritual hunger of the day to begin faith, kingdom, power, and the glory of the Lord.

In the first few centuries of Christianity, the Holy Spirit moved powerfully in signs, wonders, and miracles through God's people, turning the world upside down.

"And when they found them not, they drew Jason and certain brethren into the rulers of the city, crying, these that have turned the world upside down are come hither also" (Acts 17:6).

The Last Days' Prophetic Worshippers, Miriam Company

In the last days, there is not going to be worshiping as usual. It is going to be prophetic worship with tangible manifestations of the presence of God and divine activities. From heaven, the atmosphere of earth is the soil, but the atmosphere of heaven is glory. In the last days, when the Miriam company begins to worship, they will change the climate and the atmosphere of the church, why? It's because they will literally bring down heaven's atmosphere, which is glory.

So who is Miriam? Miriam was a woman of great courage, fearless, full of faith, a prophetess, a worshipper, a gifted leader of the people, and a truly great mother of Israel. Miriam could face her genealogy back to Adam. She was the seventh generation from Abraham. Her father was Armani, the son of Kohath, the son of Leo, the son of Jacob, the son of Isaac, the son of Abraham. Her mother was Jochebed, the daughter of Lois, the granddaughter of Isaac, and the first generation removed from

Abraham. This made Miriam the seventh generation from Abraham on her father's side and the fifth on her mother's side.

The fact is that her mother was her father's aunt. Her father married his father's sister. Jasher said that Jochebed was 126 years old when she became Arman's bride (67:1–2). We do not know how old Amram was at the time of his marriage to Jochebed, but the Bible tells us he lived to the age of 137 (Exod. 6:20).

According to Jasher, Miriam was born in the year of AM 2363 after Adam was born and the firstborn of Jochebed and Armani's children. If this is true, she would have been three years old when her brother Aaron was born and six years old when Moses was born.

At the time of Miriam's birth, the children of Israel had already been suffering as the bondslaves of Egypt. For many years Miriam would never forget those years.

Josher, in recording the history of that time, said that many of Israelites' husbands began to live celibate lives because they feared that if their wives were to become with child, they would give birth to an infant that they would have to kill. They had too much fear of God in their hearts to do such an evil deed.

Jewish tradition (the Aggadah) tells that it was because of this fear and pressure that Amran divorced his wife Jochebed.

I want to quote from the *Encyclopedia Judaica*, "The Aggadah explains that Amran, unwilling to have children who be doomed to dcarth, divorced his wife after Pharaoh's decree. Miriam urged him to remarry Jochebed, rebuking for being even crueler than Pharaoh since the latter hand decreed only against the male children, and prophesying that a child would be born from them who would be the Liberator of Israel. Amran acceded and Miriam sang and danced before her parents on the occasion of their re-marriage."

Josher, another ancient historian writes, "And it was at that time that spirit of God was upon Miriam the daughter of Amiam the sister of Aaron, she went forth and prophesied about the house, saying, Behold a son will be born unto us from my Father and mother this and he will save Israel from the land of Egypt, and when Amram heard the words of his daughter, he went and took his wife back to the house after he had driven her away at the time of Pharaoh ordered every male child of the house of Jacob to be thrown into water, three years after he had driven her away, and he came to her and she conceived" (Jasher 68:1–3).

If this is true, Miriam was a gifted prophetess from her childhood. This is entirely possible. Samuel was a prophet when he still was a child. The Bible tells us that all his prophecies came to pass (1 Sam. 3:19).

On the last days, children and their babies will prophesy. Don't be surprised! It is happening!

The amazing thing is the tremendously important role this five-year-old girl played in the deliverance and emancipation of the children of Israel from their lives of bondage in Egypt. Although God calls her a prophetess in the Bible (Exod. 15:20), none of her prophesies were recorded in the scripture. Could it be that we have to go to the ancient Jewish historical books to find why God called her a prophetess? And it was because she already started prophesying as a child? And is why Jochebed had faith that Moses would live and not die?

When reading the Bible, at first glance is hard to detect these similarities. It is only when one realizes that the Hebrew Miriam is the Greek Mary, and the Hebrew Elisheba is the Greek Elizabeth, that one can trace this revelation replay of history and the wonderful similarity to the redemption of both Israel and the world.

Truly, the ways of the Lord are marvelous as Paul writes in Roman 11:33, "O the depth of the riches both of wisdom and knowledge of God! How unsearchable are his judgements, and his ways past finding out!"

The Meaning of a Name

The naming of our children is of utmost importance because the names we give them can impact their entire lives and influences their destiny. A name is like a prophecy spoken over a child by the ones who have authority over its life. If one searches for the definition of their names of the Bible, one can discover many things concerning that person, its environment, its character, its circumstances, and its past, present, and future. It can even reveal the future of the nation (e.g., God told Hosea what to name his children). Each name had a prophetic impact on the future of Israel. If God disapproved of the names parents had given their child, he had the authority to change that name. This was what he did with Abraham and Jacob.

I have a personal tradition in our ministry that we have to dedicate any child or baby to the Lord. I must know the meaning of the child's name, so I will usually ask the parents what is the meaning of the name, and if the name doesn't have a good meaning, I will not dedicate the name of the baby is changed. And I do that because of the impact of the meaning of the name it will have on the child.

Like many Hebrew names, Miriam had a double meaning. In Hebrew, it came from the root word *meriy* which means bitter. It can be interpreted as refractory, unruly, obstinate, perverse, revly, insurrection, bitterness, affliction, sorrow, grief, and sadness. It can also mean strong, robust, vigorous, skillful. It referred to the bitterness of the bondage the people were suffering in Egypt.

Miriam was born in Egypt at a time when her people were suffering under the cruel dictatorship of a real evil ruler. On the other hand, the name Miriam could so come from the Egyptian word which means love.

Her people were suffering under the cruel dictatorship of a very evil ruler.

On the other hand, the name Miriam could also come from the Egyptian word *mer* which means love.

The title prophetess was given to her in Exodus 15:20. Miriam was the first woman to be called a prophetess in the Bible. She was first in many ways—first as a tambourine player, first female dancer, first as a woman leader in religious affairs in Israel, and the first to dare to address royalty without fear. She was precious as a child and fearless as a woman. One can usually know what a child will grow up to become by observing its childhood characteristics and personality.

In the last days, the company of Miriam, the prophetic worshippers, will hear songs from heaven and download their spirit and sing it here on earth. They will not showcase their voice; they will showcase the glory and the power of God.

They will be showcased in two realms, the natural and the supernatural at the same time.

Get ready! Get ready! The Miriam company is rising up to take thin place in these last days to fulfill God's end-time agenda and plan. Watch out! In our churches, conferences, seminars, and worship experiences we have never seen before, not only will they sin, but they will also prophesy while they worship. The Miriam company will bring the atmosphere of heaven to the earth when they begin to worship. The worship of Miriam company will give us a preview of worship in heaven. Are you one of them?

Deborah Company,
Prophetic Company

Deborah was a woman of power, authority, and honor. Her name means bee. She was a woman of unbelievable courage and wisdom, and she had faith to do the impossible and inspire others to do likewise. We do not know how old she was, but whether she was young or old, we know that she gave honor to her people in a time when they had none. She inspired men who were in the depths of despair to have hope and rise again to the greatness of courage and bravery and deliver themselves from the bondage and tyranny of one of history's most powerful and cruel tyrants that had ever ruled over an occupied nation.

She saved Israel through the gift of prophecy. Deborah will have power in the annals of history, not only as one of Israel's greatest women but as one of the greatest women of all time and all nations. For all that Deborah company, she had become an eternal role model and remind us of what God can accomplish through one of us. Just to hear her name, lifts our spirit and inspires us to have pride, confidence, faith, and courage and not to give up but to believe that God can use women to change the destiny of a nation. Deborah is the fourth judge of Israel and the only woman judge. She called herself a mother of Israel.

Now when I talked about the Deborah company, I am not talking about only women, but also men who have the spirit of Deborah as a prophetic warrior.

God's original plan was that Israel should be ruled by judges. The Lord has given instruction through his servant Moses that when they settled in the land, they were to have judges. The Lord has given instruction through his servant Moses; that was when they settled in the land and peace among the people.

"Judges and officers shalt though make the in all thy gates, which the Lord thy God giveth thee through the tribes, and they shall judge the people with just judgement. That which is altogether just shalt thou follow that thou mayest live and inherit the land which the Lord thy God giveth thee. Thou shall not plant thee a grove of any trees near unto the altar of the Lord thy God, which thou shalt make thee. Neither shalt thou set thee up any image, which the Lord thy God hateth" (Deut. 16:18–22).

The judges had the great responsibility to keep the people at peace with each other and faithfully in their worship of God.

There is a great mystery about Deborah. As I mentioned previously, her name means a bee. A bee is one of God's most precious gifts to man. It not only has the power to sting and make brave men run for their lives, but it also has the ability to make honey. The humblest bee can participate in that great achievement. Honey delights the taste and gives strength and health to the body as Gwen shall send in her wonderful book, Deborah and Jael warrior women. Dr. Thomas L. Constable in his notes on Judges 2003 edition, states, "Her name means 'bee' and she did what most marks a bee she stung the enemy, and she brought sweat refreshment to her people."

There are times when the only way that you can deliver your people is by stinging the enemy. You cannot be nice to everybody. It is an amazing story of the deliverance of Israel out of bondage. It took two gutsy and cunning women to do what the men in their day were powerless to do. Fear has them paralyzed, the men of Israel, for they regarded their enemy the Canaanites and their king Jabin, the king of the city of Jazor in Galilee and his powerful cunning commander Sisera as impossible to defeat.

The Lord of promise was a land of Milk and Honey. The Lord Himself called it that (Exod. 3:8:17, 37, 13:5, 35:3; Lev. 20:24), and this is repeated in Numbers and in Deuteronomy many times. The Lord found a woman whom He could use to restore the sweetness and the strength of the Lord.

The Greatness of Deborah

"And Deborah, a prophetess, the wife of Lapidot, she judged Israel at that time" (Judg. 4:4). According to the King James Version, we got the impression that Deborah was a married woman and that her husband name was Lapidot, but I want to draw your attention to the fact that the Hebrew word for wife, which is used here is *ishshah* (802 in Strong's Concordance, can also be interpreted woman and female). It is the same word used in Genesis 2:22–23, "And the rib, which the Lord God had taken from man, made him a woman (ishshah), and brought her unto the man, and Adam said any flesh: she shall be called woman (ishshah) because she was taken out of men (iysh)."

The word *lapidot* in Hebrew is interpreted as "to shine, lamp, flame, burning lamp, lighting, and torch." Therefore, this verse can also be interpreted—and Deborah, a prophetess, a woman as high judge of Israel at that time instead of "and Deborah, a prophetess, and the wife of Lapidot. She judged Israel at that time."

Matthew Henry's commentary on the subject says this terminology, "The wife of Lapidot is not commonly found in connection with a man. Some make this the name of a place. She was a man of Lapidot. Others take it as meaning, Lapidoth—Lamp. Some Bible scholars say she had employed herself in making wicks for the lamps of the tabernacle, and having stopped to that means office for God, or she was a woman of illuminations, or of splendors, one extra-ordinary know and wise, and so come to be very eminent and illustrious." Henry goes on to say that she was intimately acquainted with God. She was a prophetess and one that instructed others to divine knowledge by the inspiration of the spirit of God and had gifts of wisdom to which she attained not in an ordinary way. She heard the words of God and probably saw the vision of the Almighty.

She was totally devoted to Israel after Jehovah and Israel as her first love.

Deborah was a woman of lights. We can have no doubt. She was a daughter of Israel, a woman of great righteousness and excellence, who received her illumination and wisdom from the ONE WHO IS THE LIGHT OF THE WORLD that was the same LIGHT that shone in the dwelling of the Israelites back in Egypt when darkness was over all the land, and the same light gave revelation to Israel when they were in the wilderness.

The Deborah company will be men and women who are the light and walk in the light in a time and day when there is so much on every side and mankind gropes in darkness to find the way. Jesus said, "Ye are the light of the World" (Matt. 5:14).

This is the prophetic word for the last days' army of God, the undercover generation, "'Arise, shine, for thy light is come and the glory of the Lord is risen upon thee.' For behold the darkness shall cover the earth, and gross darkness of people but the Lord shall arise and his glory shall be seen upon thee. And the Gentiles shall come to thy light and kings to the brightness of their rising (Isa. 60:1–3).

In times of helplessness and hopelessness, in times of adversity, calamity, and storm, God raises movers and shakers like Deborah the prophetic warrior, Joseph Moses, Elijah, Gideon, Samson, Ester, Mary the Mother of Jesus, Winston Churchill, Abraham Lincoln, Joan of Arc, and many others.

Although it is believed by some students of ancient history that Deborah was a woman of wealth, I do not believe she was. She appeared to possess no special privileges but sat out in the open air under a palm tree, and the people came to her from all over the land to tell her about their troubles and to ask for counsel. She never charged for her counseling though it occupied much of her time. She was the one who judged the people and settled disputes among them! She was the

Solomon of her day. People respected and honored her. Her wisdom came, providing wisdom and guidance for the present and the future.

There are many things that can make one great like Deborah, and one of them was the time in which she was born. Let us look into Deborah's era.

What Caused Israel to Lese Her Greatness

Deborah lived at a time when the older generation, the pioneers and lions of faith who had all died out. They had been the ones who had seen the mighty works of God and still remembered the miracle of their deliverance from Egypt, their struggle in the howling wilderness for forty long years, their victory crossing of both the Red Sea and later the Jordan River into the promised land. Most of the time when God Almighty Himself had come down from heaven upon the great mountain in the desert and visited them, they would never forget the sound of his thunder, the roaring of the heavens, the shaking of the mountains, and the fire of his presence. They had looked down at the desert sand, standing on holy ground, and their surrounding world was the temple of God. They had seen Moses's face still shining with the glory of heaven with such a brightness that terrified them. And they had begged him to cover it lest they be blinded by its brilliance for he had been with God, and now he looked like God.

Theirs had been the generation that had such stories of miracles as men had never heard before. There was water from a rock that followed them into the wilderness, no matter where they went. There was angel's bread that dropped from the sky every morning, a mysterious cloud that led them in their journey, and a pillar of fire that covered, protected, and kept them warm through the bitterly cold winter nights, keeping their *climate* moderate at all times.

But that generation was all gone, and all this new generation doubt them and wonder if they were just a part of an imaginary, mythological past. It is true that they still had a place where they could gather to worship called the Tabernacle. It was a Shiloh and men who claimed to be descendants of one great Aaron, the first high priest, were still officiating in ceremonies that now seemed empty and without purpose. There was no partying and celebrating like the nation around them. The sad fact was that during this time of great hardship their priest and prophets were silent.

There was no prophetic word of the Lord coming from the house of the Lord at Shiloh! Where were the defenders of faith? When was the platform set for greatness in man to emerge?

Why are the spiritual leaders so often significantly silent when it is time for great men to stand up and be counted?

Is the clergy afraid to stand for truth because it might cost them a price? Did God have to use a woman under a palm tree because he couldn't find a man in his Holy Tabernacle?

The pagan neighbors, whom they had failed to drive out, were getting stronger all the time and even became friendly toward them, inviting them to their pagan festivals which enticed the soul as they filled their air with the sound of strange music they had never heard before. The brilliancy of color was everywhere. The women were free and seemed so much happier, besides they had miracles too. Their gods did strange and wondrous things for them while their own God seemed farther and farther away, and the more they went after the strange gods, the farther he seemed to withdraw from their presence. It wasn't hard to lose Him in the midst of their problems and the enticements of the world around them. Besides, it had become the acceptable thing to be broad-minded and accept other people's culture as being equal to their own.

Now and then a prophet of their faith passed through the land, warning them, and some listened and feared and went to visit the Tabernacle at Shiloh to offer sacrifices, but for the most part, nobody paid much need to these offensive old men who made them uncomfortable.

This was a generation that not only was forsaking their God but was also forgetting the great truth that He has given them into the book of the law.

This was a generation which "knew not the Lord, not yet the works which he had done for Israel" (Judg. 2:10).

The Prophetic Warrior

No one knew the hearts of the people better than Deborah. As they came to her with their pains, their sorrows, their broken hearts, and the burdens of their transgression and their guilt, they would confess their sins to her. She knew the heart of Israel. She became an intercessor for her people. There were many nights when, after a long day of comforting, exhorting, correcting, and praying for her people, she would weep in their darkness of the night for God to have mercy on Israel and send deliverance.

No one is qualified to carry the responsibility of government as the one who has wept and prayed for victory at the throne room of heaven! Day after day she saw and heard about the wretched state of the people as they showed her their wounds and the terrible scars of their beatings. Fathers told how their wives and young daughters have been shamefully and viciously abused, their sons tortured and killed in front of their eyes, and many other things too cruel to write about. This happened year after the year for twenty long years, and as time went by, things only worsened under the oppressive cruelty of King Jabin until finally "his cups of iniquity was full." This time when Israel cried out to God in depression for divine intervention, God said enough.

He spoke to Deborah and told her to send her Barak, the son of Abinoam, who was living in Kedesh-Naphtali about four miles from the north end of the Water of Meroth

Why Deborah Company

Through the years, many men have asked, "Why did God choose a woman? Why didn't he choose a man as his prophet in those perilous times?" I believe it was for two reasons. One, God can choose whomsoever He will. Two, it was because Deborah was a woman the enemy would never suspect—how great a threat she was to his evil schemes. The Deborah company is unassuming and the enemy cannot figure them out. As a result, he underestimated them for their power, prophetic insight, and their ability. He did not dream that a woman would lead the people, whom he kept in oppressive enslavement, in a *way of liberation*. Someone has said that women are God's secret weapons! (He chooses the foolish things to confound the wise).

The place where she lived is in close proximity where another Deborah was buried, the nurse of Rebekah who had died and was buried under a great oak tree (Gen. 35:8). It was here, at Bethel, that Jacob had met with God as he fled from his brother Esau. Here, in a dream, the Lord had shown him a ladder that reached from the earth to heaven which caused him to call the place Bethel (the house of God). Much later on his return to the land of Mesopotamia, Jacob and his family had a very important meeting with God. They got rid of all their idiots and made a fresh dedication of their lives to him. After all these years, Bethel was still the house of God, and the presence of God was still there. God still met with his people there and spoke to them. Certain places on earth are anointed by God, and even after many years, one can still feel the presence of God there. So it is at the Western Wall in Jerusalem.

The Bible says that the first Deborah, the nurse of Rebekah, was buried under an oak tree (Gen. 35:8). This Deborah dwelt under a palm tree. Palm trees are known for their deep roots. They can survive strong storms which would uproot, break, or destroy even strong oaks! A palm tree's strength is in its roots ad its flexibility to bend with the forces of the storm.

A great leader must have the qualifications. The opposition will never have the power to uproot those whose convictions are anchored because they have an inner strength that is hidden from the world. A great leader will also have the ability to appear to yield under pressure but will actually bounce right back up when things calm down again.

Such a person was Deborah our prophetess. She had the ability to survive the storms that threatened her people from the wicked

Canaanites in Northern Galilee. It is believed by many scholars that she was a daughter of the tribe of Issachar. This made it twice as hard to endure steadfastly in her calling because it was in her trial area that the enemy had firmly entrenched himself and overtaken the land. He was on every hand. We were always watching, spying, and getting people in trouble, but his presence did not daunt her because the presence of the Lord was like a bubble around her. She had her own personal *cloud by day and pillar of fire by night*. She lived in the Shekinah of the Rugh Ha Kodesh. That was why was the title the woman of light.

Israel knew that Deborah was a woman sent by God. They knew this about John the Baptist too (John 1:6) just because the religious leaders of his day did not recognize or accept him. They did not disqualify him from his high calling. John had the authority of heaven, and Deborah did too. They were both qualified to speak in the name of God.

Deborah was an extraordinary prophetess who understood the times and knew the mind and counsel of God. The last days' prophetic company of Deborah will not make a more unless God that spoken, will not engage the enemy unless God asks them to, and when they receive a prophetic signal to do anything, nothing stops them. This is a prophetic oil that flows constantly; it never goes dry.

When Barak was told by Deborah to come, he immediately knew in his heart that this was not a call from a woman; it was a call from the Almighty!

His heart was racing as he traveled on foot from the tribe of Naphtali to the territory of the tribe of Issachar, the very heart of the enemy occupation. Most of us would have sent excuses! But he was buried in the place of the palm tree where the great mother of Israel spoke the oracles of God to her people.

When he stood before her, she did not command him. She asked him if he had heard God speak to his heart, "Hath not the Lord God of Israel commanded, saying, Go and draw towards Mount Tablor, and take with thee then thousand men of the children of Naphtali and of the children of Zebulon" (Judg. 4:6).

Most of the time, when we receive a prophecy through someone, it is a confirmation of something that the Lord has already spoken to us. When that happens, it is time to sit up and take notice.

Deborah knew that God had spoken to him and had even told him about a fire battle. That is one of the wonderful things about the gift of prophecy; it is usually a confirmation of something that God has already spoken. It is a confirmation of what the heart already knows, and Deborah knew that God has already called Barak to the battle. So he just needed this extra *prophetic shove*.

As she looked at this young, handsome son of the tribe of Naphtali standing before her. She didn't just see on the outside, she could see right into his heart. She knew what the Lord has spoken to him before he ever arrived. It was as though she had heard all that God has said to him and how he had dealt with his heart. Let us go back with Deborah into the background which was not recorded in our Bible. I can visualize Barak, that son of the tribe of Naphtali, as he sits, hiding in his den or cave and God is speaking to him, telling him that he has been chosen to lead the children of Israel to battle against their powerful enemy, the destroyer of their land and their lives.

Barak considered his youth, he lived an inexperienced life and empty hands, and he thought that he must be crazy to imagine that he could do anything to save Israel from so powerful an enemy. He shook his head and said to himself, "How could I tell anyone that God has chosen me to raise an army to liberate us from our bondage? No one would ever believe me. It is impossible. I must be crazy. Besides, we don't even have one single weapon of any kind in all of Israel. We are defenseless."

How many of us, have a hard time believing that God can use us in a great way! We feel so small and useless, but we must take our eyes off ourselves and put them on the Lord. It is not our strength or our talents that will save the day; it is the almighty power of our Almighty God. Abraham was just the "saint of amour" that God wore when He went to battle against His enemy who has blasphemed Him and enticed His people to worship false gods. Every battle, He just lets us have the honor of getting the credit for it.

How would he do it as Barak stood there looking at the mother of Israel. He shifted his legs uneasily because he knew she was "reading his mail."

"Barak, son of Abinoam," she begins, "hasn't the Lord God of Israel commanded you what he wants you to do?"

It seemed to him as though her eyes pierced through his soul. He couldn't deny it.

Then she began to give him military instruction for warfare and prophesied what the results would be, "Go and draw toward Mount Tabo, and take with thee ten thousand men of the children of Zebulun. And I Jehovah will draw unto thee to the river Kishon fifera, the captain of Jabin's army, and I will deliver him into thine hand" (Judg. 4:6b–7).

As he heard the prophetess tell him the secret of God which he had kept hidden in his heart, he knew it was a confirmation of what he had felt but had told no one. I can imagine how shaken he was when Deborah looked him straight in the eye and told him the thing he was hoping was only a foolish notion, in turn, was the call of God upon his life. He thought, "This is too big of a responsibility for me. I am not qualified for the task. God needs some great champion, a lion of Judah, not a Naphtali!"

Not only did she know that God had called Barak to lead His people to the war of liberation, she saw by the spirit, the military strategy that God wanted him to use.

There is no doubt that the reason Israel has never lost a battle in all its history because they get their military intelligence from a higher *military pentagon* than the one in Washington DC. His war plans can never fail. The commander in chief of this army knows how to fight His own battles.

King Jabin's soldiers were scattered throughout the region, but God promised that He would draw them out to the River Kishon, where they would expose themselves and that when God got them all together in one place, He Himself would hand them over into the hands of Israel under the command of His general Barak. What a sure positive promise of victory!

The Last Days

The Anna Prophetic Company

A new breed of people is rising up called according to the pattern of Anne. They are prophetic intercessors, the watchmen and women that battle and war on their knees. This prophetic company doesn't have affluence but has influence. They may not have monetary and political influence, but they have spiritual influence. The Anna prophetic company takes hold of the word and what God has said through prophecy, and they pray it into main fruition.

Beloved, let me tell you a prophetic fact, heaven is ready to invade the earth with the unmarked, undeniable power of God, such as we have never seen in the book of Acts, biblical and church history. The church is on the horizon of great awakening and unusual revival filled with the gloriousness of God.

God doesn't operate in a vacuum that is why the Anna anointing and mantle is being released to the last days' army.

The Anna company is a company of prophetic prayer and fasting in preparation.

"But if they are prophets, and if the word of the Lord is with them, let them now make intercession to the Lord of hosts, that the vessels which are left in the house of the Lord, in the house of the King of Judah, and at Jerusalem, to not go to Babylon" (Jer. 27:18, NKJV).

These prophetic intercessors will be dreaded by the kingdom of Satan because they will silence the voice of the accuser and destroy the works of Satan and his lords of demons.

Get ready. You are part of this army. You have been enlisted, trained, and prepared for such a time as this.

"For thus hath the Lord said unto me, 'Go, set a watchman, let him declare what he seeth'" (Isa. 21:6, KJV).

"But the end of all things is at hand: be ye therefore sober, and watch unto prayer" (1 Pet. 4:7, KJV).

The author Raphael Grant can be contacted through his websites eagleschapel.com or raphaelgrant.com. For bookings, you may call (770) 941-1934.

To write the author:

3100 Joe Jerkins Blvd.

Austell, Ga 30106

Email:

grantaretha@gmail.com